At Issue

Is the Political Divide Harming America?

Other books in the At Issue series:

At Issue

Is the Political Divide Harming America?

Julia Bauder, Book Editor

GREENHAVEN PRESS

An imprint of Thomson Gale, a part of The Thomson Corporation

THOMSON
™
GALE

Detroit • New York • San Francisco • San Diego • New Haven, Conn.
Waterville, Maine • London • Munich

THOMSON

✦

™

GALE

Bonnie Szumski, *Publisher*
Helen Cothran, *Managing Editor*

© 2006 Thomson Gale, a part of The Thomson Corporation.

Thomson and Star logo are trademarks and Gale and Greenhaven Press are registered trademarks used herein under license.

For more information, contact:
Greenhaven Press
27500 Drake Rd.
Farmington Hills, MI 48331-3535
Or you can visit our Internet site at http://www.gale.com

LIBRARY OF CONGRESS CATALOGING-IN-PUBLICATION DATA

Is the political divide harming America? / Julia Bauder, book editor
    p. cm. -- (At issue)
  Includes bibliographical references and index.
  0-7377-3521-X (lib. : alk. paper) 0-7377-3522-8 (pbk. : alk. paper)
    1. Polarization (Social sciences) 2. Political parties--United States. 3. United States--Politics and government--2001. I. Bauder, Julia. II. At issue (San Diego, Calif.)
  HN90.P57I8 2006
  973.93--dc22

        2006041175

Printed in the United States of America
10 9 8 7 6 5 4 3 2 1

Contents

Introduction

According to many political observers, a new age in American political history opened on November 7, 2000. That was a presidential election day, and for the first time in twenty years when Election Day dawned the outcome of the vote was still very much in doubt. The Democratic ticket, then–Vice President Al Gore and Senator Joe Lieberman, and the Republicans, Texas governor George W. Bush and former secretary of defense Dick Cheney, were running neck and neck in opinion polls, and as many as a dozen states were still considered to be toss-ups.

At midnight that night, after the polls had closed, the outcome was no clearer. Twenty-nine states with 246 electoral votes had clearly gone to Bush and Cheney, while Gore and Lieberman were sitting on 255 electoral votes gained from sixteen states and the District of Columbia. Three states were too close to call: New Mexico, with five electoral votes; Oregon, with seven; and Florida, with twenty-five. The only way either set of candidates could reach the 270 electoral votes necessary for victory was by taking Florida.

Thus began a thirty-five-day-long battle of lawsuits, as both sides tried to use the legal system to gain an advantage in Florida's recount process. While teams of lawyers for the two candidates argued inside courthouses across Florida, protesters outside held signs proclaiming Gore to be a "Sore Loserman" and declaring that "Bush/Cheated"—signs modeled after the two sides' respective campaign logos.

Finally, on December 12, 2000, the U.S. Supreme Court ordered a halt to all recounts in Florida, effectively handing the election to Bush, who was ahead in the current count. However, a hard core of Democratic activists continued to maintain that Gore had actually won the election and that Bush's victory was illegitimate. Some argued that Bush's younger brother, Florida governor Jeb Bush, had conspired to manipulate the election; others placed the blame with Supreme Court justices nominated by former Republican presidents including Bush's father, George H.W. Bush. Even those who accepted the results of the election as legal noted that Bush was the first president since 1888 to win in the electoral college without winning the popular vote—over half a million more people nationwide voted for Gore than voted for Bush.

Resentment over Bush's narrow victory in 2000, fortified by anger over his controversial decision to go to war in Iraq in 2003 based on what was later proven to be faulty intelligence, carried over into the 2004 presidential election, which pitted Bush against Massachusetts senator John Kerry. This resentment led to numerous acts of vandalism and minor violence in the days leading up to the election. In two of the most notable incidents, a group of protesters stormed a Bush/Cheney election headquarters in Orlando, Florida; and several people, allegedly including the sons of two Democratic politicians, slashed the tires on twenty-five vans that Wisconsin Republicans had planned to use to take voters to the polls on Election Day.

Once again, as the day of the election neared, opinion polls showed the two candidates effectively tied. Anticipating a repeat of the close 2000 vote, Bush and Kerry between them had over forty thousand lawyers working around the country in the days before the election. These attorneys filed lawsuits to have the election conducted on terms favorable to their candidates and prepared additional suits to be filed if they perceived slights to their sides' would-be voters. Once again when midnight arrived several states were still too close to call, and it looked as if more suits would soon start flying.

This time the election would come down to Ohio, where early results showed Bush with a potentially beatable lead of over one hundred thousand votes. However, as the night went on it became clear that the odds of Kerry being able to win the state were slim. The next morning he conceded and called for national unity, reminding his supporters that "in an American election there are no losers, because whether or not our candidates are successful, the next morning we all wake up as Americans."

Despite Kerry's plea for reconciliation, many Americans still felt like they lived in a divided country. Some, with varying degrees of seriousness, even called for the country to be formally divided. A popular graphic circulating on the World Wide Web in the days following the 2004 election showed a map of North America with the Pacific Coast, Northeast, and Great Lakes states that voted for Kerry merged with Canada and renamed the "United States of Canada," while the remaining states, those that supported Bush, were declared "Jesusland." Other frustrated Kerry supporters wrote manifestos calling for the creation of a new country, "Coastopia," which would contain the Pacific Coast states, the Northeast, and a few other areas, or, more seriously, for an "Urban Archipelago" of Democratic-controlled cities that would not formally secede but would isolate themselves from the surrounding Republican suburbs and rural areas.

These calls for secession were mostly jokes, but, like much humor, they were popular because they tapped into strong emotions that many people were experiencing. Some observers fear that, if these trends continue, the desire for liberal and conservative Americans to separate from each other could become serious and the essential unity of the United States could be endangered. In fact, some people believe that this is already happening. Others argue that these concerns have been blown out of proportion and that the American political system remains healthy and strong. These are the issues debated by the authors in *At Issue: Is the Political Divide Harming America?*

1

America's Political Divide Is Deep

David Von Drehle

David Von Drehle is a staff writer for the Washington Post.

American voters are increasingly divided into two distinct political camps that identify strongly with the major parties. This division has many causes, including increasing ideological purity in the political parties, new technologies that allow candidates to target their campaigns to narrow subgroups, and increasing segregation of Republicans and Democrats into separate geographic communities. All of these factors are causing politics to become more bitter and polarized.

[1994 to 2004 was] one of the most eventful [decades] in American political history. . . . And yet, like a bathroom scale springing back to zero, the electorate keeps returning to near-parity. It's happening again: A little more than six months before Election Day [2004], numerous polls find President [George W.] Bush in a very tight race with Democratic challenger Sen. John F. Kerry among a sharply divided electorate. A large number of voters—seven in 10, according to one Pew Research Center poll—say they have already made up their minds and cannot be swayed.

Causes of the Political Divide

What explains it? From Congress to the airwaves to the best-seller lists, American politics appears to be hardening into un-

David Von Drehle, "Political Spirit Is Pervasive: Clash of Cultures Is Driven by Targeted Appeals and Reinforced by Geography," *Washington Post*, April 25, 2004.

compromising camps, increasingly identified with the two parties. According to a growing consensus of political scientists, demographers and strategists, the near-stalemate of 2000—which produced a virtual tie for the White House, a 50-50 Senate and a narrow Republican edge in the House of Representatives—was no accident.

This split is nurtured by the marketing efforts of the major parties, which increasingly aim pinpoint messages to certain demographic groups, rather than seeking broadly appealing new themes. It is reinforced by technology, geography and strategy. And now it is driving the presidential campaign, and explains why many experts anticipate a particularly bitter and divisive [2004] election.

Like a bathroom scale springing back to zero, the electorate keeps returning to near-parity.

Political scientists and practitioners often speak of "Red-Blue America," evoking maps of the 2000 election returns; indeed, the phrase is used so loosely that it has spawned a competing pundit class devoted to knocking down oversimplifications of the idea. . . .

It's useful to examine the Red-Blue division—what it is, where it came from, how it has deepened and what it might mean.

Ideological Sorting

Hans Noel, a political scientist at the University of California at Los Angeles, is the author of a paper called "The Road to Red and Blue America." In an interview, he said, "Most people say they are 'moderate,' but in fact the country is polarized around strong conservative and liberal positions." For the first time in generations, he said, those philosophical lines correspond to party lines. The once-hardy species of conservative Democrats—so numerous in the 1980s they had a name, "Reagan Democrats"—is now on the endangered list, along with the liberal "Rockefeller Republicans."

"It has taken 40 or 50 years to work itself out, but the ideological division in America—which is not new—is now lined up with the party division," Noel said.

At the same time, more and more Americans in a highly mobile society are choosing to live among like-minded people. University of Maryland political demographer James Gimpel has documented the rise of a "patchwork nation," in which political like attracts like, and ideologically diverse communities are giving way to same-thinking islands. A recent analysis sponsored by the *Austin American-Statesman*, comparing the photo-finish elections of 1976 and 2000, made this clear. While the nationwide results were extremely close, nearly twice as many voters now live in counties where one candidate or the other won by a landslide. Person by person, family by family, America is engaging in voluntary political segregation.

Bush and Kerry embody the role of mobility and personal choices in creating the Red-Blue nation. Two Establishment scions, similar in background and education, who parted ways after being at Yale University together, one headed to Red country and the other to Blue. Millions of voters have now made similar choices, which in turn echo and reinforce their initial beliefs and preferences.

As John Kenneth White, author of *The Values Divide*, put it in an interview, "The reds get redder and blues get bluer."

Sharper Divisions

This reality is already visible in the presidential campaign. Kerry supporters routinely attack Bush with the familiar Red stereotypes—he is, according to the charges, ignorant, belligerent, a cowboy, a religious zealot. Likewise, Bush supporters brand Kerry as elitist, a snob, lacking conviction and unpatriotic.

Onto those stereotypes the campaigns have begun layering issues well-known for firing up the Red and Blue camps: taxes, gay rights, abortion and the United Nations, to name a few. Occasional speeches may pay homage to broad, unifying themes, but the campaign day to day seems intended to deepen, rather than erase, the rift. This suggests candidates resigned to a tight finish. Indeed, Bush political chief Karl Rove has predicted a razor-thin margin in the 2004 race almost from Day One of the administration, never wavering even when his candidate was riding near-record approval ratings.

Person by person, family by family, America is engaging in voluntary political segregation.

Twenty years ago, Republican President Ronald Reagan swept 49 states in his reelection landslide. Today, the sheer number of voters who already tell pollsters they will not consider voting for Bush suggests how difficult it would be to win that sort of broad mandate. Instead, strategists for Bush and Kerry are focused on a short list of hard-fought states.

As it becomes more difficult to reach across the party line, campaigns are devoting more energy to firing up their hardcore supporters. For voters in the middle, [the 2004] election may aggravate their feeling that politics no longer speaks to them, that it has become a dialogue of the deaf, a rant of uncompromising extremes.

Finally, because the Red-Blue divide so often follows very personal values—matters of philosophy, spirituality, morals and taste—the coming election appears primed to leave the losing faction not just disappointed, but angry. There's a reason why the last two presidents, Bill Clinton and George W. Bush, have driven their opposition into fits of loathing: Politics in Red-Blue America is less the art of compromise than a clash of cultures.

Parallel Universes

The Red-Blue thesis has a range of critics, from well-read sophisticates in Red zones who resent being stereotyped to liberals who feel the framework unfairly portrays them as cut off from Main Street America. Some critics feel the model wrongly avoids talking about the millions of eligible citizens who don't show up as either color, because they don't vote.

Actually, Red zones and Blue zones are demographically similar in many ways. Lots of Red voters live in Blue country, and vice versa. Gallup pollsters have emphasized what they call "purple states," a geographically diverse atlas in which the total votes cast for Bush and Vice President Al Gore in 2000 produced a statistical deadlock: Florida, Iowa, Minnesota, Missouri, Nevada, New Hampshire, New Mexico, Ohio, Oregon, Pennsylvania, Tennessee and Wisconsin.

The notion of two tribes unhappily sharing a country is gaining strength among analysts, however. "It's huge," Noel said. "People in these two countries don't even see each other." And that's partly because of political segregation.

Consider the 1960 presidential election—another virtual dead heat. Democrat John F. Kennedy captured states in nearly every region of the country. By contrast, in 2000 Democrat Gore was shut out of the South, the Plains states and—with the exception of New Mexico—the Rocky Mountain West.

To an extent not seen in generations, the political parties occupy distinct philosophical spaces.

The states Gore picked up from the 1960 Republican column were likewise concentrated in certain regions: the West Coast, the Great Lakes and New England.

America's Political Divide Is Deep

According to a recent survey by pollster John Zogby, voters in states that went for Bush were, by clear statistical margins, older, more likely to be married, less likely to join a union, more likely to be regular churchgoers—mostly at Protestant churches—and far more likely to be "born again" Christians.

Another prominent opinion sampler, Stanley B. Greenberg, has made similar findings. Blue Americans, he concluded, are most likely to be found among highly educated women, non-churchgoers, union members and the "cosmopolitans" of the New York area, New England and California.

"We have two parallel universes," White said. "Each side seeks to reinforce its thinking by associating with like-minded people."

Philosophical Differences

But Red-Blue is not just a matter of place. To an extent not seen in generations, the political parties occupy distinct philosophical spaces. There's scant room left in national politics for a liberal Republican or a conservative Democrat—just ask Sen. James M. Jeffords [Independent], the former Republican from Vermont, or Sen. Zell Miller, a pro-Bush Democrat from Georgia. A generation ago, such figures were crucial to congressional deal-making. Now, they are ostracized.

"I think it's more of a chasm" than a divide, Jeffords said in an e-mail. "There's very little room for moderate voices. . . . They are being silenced by the extremes. Three years ago, when I left the Republican Party, I said the president was moving too far to the right. I think he's proven me right, and now we've got gridlock."

Miller, who has leveled similar complaints against the Democratic leadership, declined to be interviewed.

Collapsed Coalition

Factions are nothing new. Most of the ideological rifts in American politics today can be traced back over centuries:

15

North vs. South, rural vs. urban, populist vs. elitist, labor vs. ownership, religious vs. secular.

But those rifts haven't always coincided with party divisions. The United States was led for many years by the strange bedfellows of Franklin D. Roosevelt's New Deal coalition. Millions of rural, religious, southern voters joined millions of urban, minority and secular voters in backing the Democrats. After Roosevelt's death and World War II, the coalition began fragmenting—over civil rights and anti-communism, among other issues—but the breakup took decades.

Experts cite a variety of factors to explain why Red-Blue has risen in its place. For example:

[Ronald] Reagan happened. Republican presidents Dwight D. Eisenhower, Richard M. Nixon and Gerald R. Ford governed essentially as pragmatic centrists, but Reagan framed his presidency in ideological terms. He coaxed religious conservatives and Cold Warriors away from the Democratic Party while making it uncomfortable for liberals to remain in the GOP. "The signals coming out from Washington helped voters sort themselves out into parties that reflected their world view," explained Thomas E. Mann of the Brookings Institution.

Peace happened. From the outbreak of World War II through the end of the Cold War—a span of nearly 50 years—the United States' foreign policy and military policy, two of the biggest responsibilities of the government, reflected the consensus of both parties. "In the 1950s, the country thought of itself as homogenous," said White, recalling sociologist Daniel Bell's influential 1960 book, *The End of Ideology.* "The dominant discussion was about the need for unity in the face of a potent enemy." The collapse of the Soviet Union stripped much of the purpose out of centrism.

Clinton happened. Though he campaigned as a moderate Democrat, and delivered on such longtime Republican goals as a balanced budget and welfare reform, Clinton's administration ultimately proved highly divisive. The first baby boomer presidency opened a new front in the culture wars that erupted in the late 1960s—over sex, responsibility, the role of women, the nature of authority.

Technology happened. The rise of direct mail, cable television and the Internet has enabled ideological soul mates to find one another efficiently, to organize, to concentrate their resources and to evangelize. Big Media—especially network television and daily newspapers—are rapidly losing their power to shape public consensus and marginalize ideological extremes.

The Pew Research Center for the People and the Press recently found that the number of Americans getting campaign news from network television or daily newspapers has fallen by a quarter since 2000, and by a third for magazines such as *Time* and *Newsweek*. Meanwhile, the audience is growing for niche outlets such as talk radio, cable television and Internet sites.

"People naturally reduce cognitive dissonance by seeking out information that reinforces their existing views," Mann said. "So there's no single cause" of the Red-Blue divide, "but a number of factors feeding into this."

50 Percent Plus One

Some political scientists add another factor: simple political self-interest. According to the influential economic analysis known as "game theory," logic may compel the parties to aim for the narrowest possible victory margin.

"In a democracy, to win you need a majority," UCLA's Noel said. "But you don't want a lot *more* than 50-percent-plus-one, because if your majority gets bigger, you have to share the spoils with more supporters. That's no good. So the natural process is to produce division."

He continued: "If you look at the 2000 election, the divisions by state are pretty lopsided. But nationally, you get pretty close to a 50-50 split. That shouldn't be a surprise, because that's what these forces are designed for."

An example of this was the decision by the parties after the 2000 U.S. Census to agree on new congressional districts that left 90 percent or more of the seats safely Red or Blue. This severely limits the chance that either party will develop a large congressional majority.

It has also further entrenched the ideological standoff. As Mann explained, few House incumbents now have any incentive to reach across party lines to win general elections. Once they have their party's nomination, the lopsided districting virtually guarantees they will win. So the pressure is on them to toe the ideological line to avoid primary election challenges.

The Archetypal Red Candidate

Now the Republicans and Democrats have produced perfect archetypes of Red and Blue as their presidential nominees.

Bush and Kerry started adult life from virtually the same spot: as well-bred, prep-school products who could be found, in 1965 and 1966, at Yale. Their fathers were in public service, and both young men sensed, to one degree or another, that they would follow. True, one came from a long line of Republicans and the other from a family of Democrats. But one of the functions of their exclusive training, according to author Kai Bird, was to prepare future leaders to govern in pragmatic, bipartisan ways.

The crucial question in any election is, "Do the voters think the candidates are people like them?"

After graduation, however, their paths diverged. Bush left New England to live in Midland, Tex. He entered the oil business—in which extracting resources was valued above conservation, regulation was seen as an affront to enterprise and everything depended on the readiness of bold men to take big risks. Texas was part of the Wild West, the Old Confederacy and the Bible Belt.

In short, Bush immersed himself in a Red sea. Greenberg, author of *The Two Americas: Our Current Political Deadlock and How to Break It*, recently summed up the essence of that world.

"Faith in God and faith in entrepreneurs," Greenberg said. "The idea that faith should inform our public space, and that absolutes, rooted in the Bible, should guide us in our public life. The idea that America should be strong in promoting freedom and in control of our own destiny. Texas is actually a lot more complicated than that—but not where Bush lives."

When Bush extols "entrepreneurs," insists on tax cutting and deregulation, and promotes drilling and logging; when he professes a born-again faith and appeals to traditional norms on issues such as marriage and cloning; when he disdains intellectual subtleties in favor of plain-spoken verities, he is carrying the flag for Red America.

The Archetypal Blue Candidate

Kerry went another way. After winning medals in Vietnam, he launched into the culturally progressive, antiwar politics of the East Coast. In Kerry's world, liberal values were worth paying for with higher taxes. There was less talk about celebrating entrepreneurs than about reining in "corporate interests." Kerry's Boston milieu was Yankee North and ivory tower, a magnet for the young and the wealthy, many of whom saw urban life as a model of multicultural America.

Again, Greenberg's data confirm that these broad generalizations—while imperfect—rest on a foundation in reality.

"Kerry chose a very cosmopolitan part of the country, globally connected," he said. "It is less comfortable with absolutes. One's faith provides personal guidance, but people are somewhat uncomfortable about applying this to civil society. Self-expression is a central value. Boston seems as much a ground zero to postmodernist Blue America as Midland is to Red America."

Kerry hoists the Blue flag whenever he embraces environmentalism, labor unionism and regulation; when he emphasizes the complexities of issues and urges an internationalist foreign policy; when he gives precedence to tolerance over tradition and dissent over conformity.

Both men try, at least in symbolic ways, to reach for the center. Bush reads to schoolchildren and preaches "love your neighbors"—symbols of a warm, "compassionate" side to his conservative stances on taxes and morality. Kerry rides a Harley and speaks often of his combat days—symbols of toughness amid his internationalism and social liberalism.

But their basic colors show through.

Veteran political analyst Ben Wattenberg said the crucial question in any election is, "Do the voters think the candidates are people like them?" [In 2004], that question will be asked by two very different sorts of people, by a political system intent on pushing them apart.

America's Political Divide Is Exaggerated

Michael Robinson and Susan Ellis

Michael Robinson retired from the government department at Georgetown University in 1993 and serves as a consultant to the Pew Research Center, a nonpartisan research organization that specializes in trends and attitudes in America. Susan Ellis is a senior analyst at Market Strategies, Inc., a research and consulting firm in Livonia, Michigan.

America is not as politically divided as the media and politicians of both parties claim. Many southern and Sun Belt states that voted for Republican George W. Bush in 2000 have Democratic governors, and several northeastern and Pacific states that voted for Democrat Al Gore have Republican governors. These mixed results suggest that individual voters are willing to support candidates from both parties. Consistent with this conclusion, many more voters describe themselves as politically "moderate" than as "very conservative" or "very liberal." Voters may split fifty-fifty in presidential elections, but this does not mean that the electorate is polarized. It merely means that both parties are competitive.

On June 1 [2004], Stephanie Herseth, a true-blue Democrat, won a special election for the lone House seat in the blood-red state of South Dakota. But in a state that gave George Bush 60 percent of its vote back in 2000, Herseth's win turns out to be the rule, not the exception. The two senators from South Dakota are also Democrats. Political "blue flu" infects both Dakotas. North Dakota also elects one House member along with its two senators. Again, all three are Democrats, even though Bush did even better in North Dakota than in South.

Two blood-red states. Six true-blue congressional Democrats. Not a Republican in sight. How can this be happening in a political environment that is assumed to be polarized state by state, region by region? The answer is that the assumption is wrong. The theory of red states versus blue states is about as wide of the mark as it is widely accepted.

Mix of Red and Blue

From the Capitol dome, one can look east into blue Maryland. But Maryland has a red governor. One can look west and see a reddish Virginia; but Virginia has a bluish chief executive. Climb down from the Capitol and travel west by southwest, through the American version of the Red Belt. Let's see how far one can go into the Red Belt and still find blue governors. Travel down toward Tennessee: blue governor. Cross the Mississippi into Missouri: blue governor. Then take your pick: Kansas or Oklahoma—two longtime red states, both with recently elected blue governors.

Drive the Oklahoma panhandle into the Sun Belt, which for 40 years has been considered not just sunny but solidly Republican. And yet once-red New Mexico now has a very blue governor, Bill Richardson. End up in Arizona, what was once Goldwater[1] country and is still color-coded bright red on The Map. Arizona also has a new governor who is blue. California is blue, so we won't, as the Californians say, go there. But even Valley Girls know that California just installed as chief executive Arnold Schwarzenegger—a man of many colors.

1. Barry Goldwater was an influential conservative Republican who served as senator from Arizona between 1953 and 1987.

And what about the other blue states? Are they as faithless to their party as the red states we just visited? In a word, yes. Al Gore wound up winning only three states by 20 points or more: Rhode Island, Massachusetts, and New York. All three have Republican governors. In fact, New York has not elected a Democratic governor since Mario Cuomo in 1990; Massachusetts hasn't elected a Democrat to its top office since Michael Dukakis in 1986; Rhode Island hasn't elected a Democratic governor for 14 years. Indeed, seven of the ten states Al Gore won by the largest majorities all currently have Republican governors.

The theory of red states versus blue states is about as wide of the mark as it is widely accepted.

For those who prefer something a bit more systematic than a travelogue, we have checked all 50 states for loyalty to their color. Every state has at least three offices elected statewide: the governor and the two senators. A polarized state in a polarized nation, you might think, would commonly show all three officials either red or blue. Yet [as of 2004] only 16 states have a political triumvirate that is monochromatic and matches the state's Campaign 2000 color. Thirty-three states fail the test; their statewide elected leadership is a mix of red and blue. The 50th state is unique. George W. Bush didn't break a sweat to win in hot and humid Louisiana in 2000, but in 2004 all three statewide leaders are Democrats.

Voters Are Mostly Moderate

So much for the states. What about The People? The best way to answer that question is to ask them. No pollster with any sense would ask people whether they see themselves as polarized. Terminology like that is Greek to them. But pollsters do ask voters to describe themselves politically. The Pew Research Center has been doing just that for more than a dozen years.

Pew asks, "In general, would you describe yourself as very conservative, conservative, moderate, liberal, or very liberal?" In May of [2004], a meager 5 percent labeled themselves "very conservative." The exact same percentage said "very liberal." Forty-one percent said "moderate." So there are *four* times as many moderates as "wingers"—right or left.

What about in years past? Consider the politically charged year of 1994, when Newt Gingrich rose from obscurity to become the first Republican speaker of the House in four decades. The numbers from 1994 are virtually identical with those from 2004. The wings accounted for 10 percent of the public at large; the moderate category contained 39 percent of the total. After ten eventful years, there's been no change in how and where the public positions itself. The watchword then and now is centrism.

Pundits and political scientists have equated "evenly divided" with "polarized." Big mistake.

Pew's most recent and wide-ranging study of polarization, completed in 2003, finds that Democrats and Republicans now differ more widely on issues and values than at any time in the last 15 years. Fair enough. But we checked the 50-plus items that Pew included in that survey and found the nation as a whole was not closely divided on most issues and values. In fact, about a quarter of all those questions indicated a public closely divided, while there was something approaching national consensus on a third of them.

Politicians know all this, even if the conventional wisdom doesn't. Why else would George W. Bush have strained to pass the largest entitlement package in 40 years? Why else would John Kerry now oppose gay marriage and favor an additional 40,000 soldiers for the Army? They do all this because each realizes that for the vast majority of Americans extremism is still a vice, and moderation is still a virtue.

Evenly Divided, Not Polarized

Why, then, the obsession with polarization? The most important reason is an error in logic. Pundits and political scientists have equated "evenly divided" with "polarized." Big mistake.

In 1860, one-third of the states were on their way to becoming the Confederacy. Two-thirds would remain in the Union. America was not equally divided then, but she was most certainly polarized. In 1960, Americans were evenly divided, at least as to presidential preference. Yet Americans were not especially polarized at the time. So, taken together, 1860 and 1960 prove that being evenly divided is neither a necessary nor sufficient condition for polarization.

There's a serious definition problem here as well. Polarization is not a modest increase in differences between Democrats and Republicans. That definition is both myopic and alarmist. Polarization worthy of the name involves an intensity and hostility that engenders some level of political violence, or something akin to it. At minimum, real polarization must produce an extremist movement with significant public support.

Think 1968. Remember the ugliness of George Wallace's Independent party, a backlash movement that attracted nearly 10 million very hostile voters, and even garnered 46 votes in the Electoral College. Compared with Wallace voters, Ralph Nader's 3 million voters in 2000 are few in number and very bourgeois. Political grievances in the past have spawned the [Ku Klux] Klan, the SDS [Students for a Democratic Society], and the Nation of Islam. Political grievances since 2000 have given us the "Deaniacs" [supporters of 2004 presidential election candidate Howard Dean]. The 1860s and the late 1960s epitomized genuine political polarization. The "50-50" politics of this decade do not.

Misleading Map

Then there is the tyranny of "Map 2000"—the unfortunate byproduct of Electoral College realities and television's ongoing standard operating procedures. In the Electoral College, the states matter far more than the voters. In television journalism, the visuals matter way too much. It was great for television that the blue states and the red states seemed to be oh-so-regionalized. But we have been color-blinded by The Map.

The best example is the West Coast. TV's uniformly bright-blue coloring of Oregon, Washington, and California implied that the coast was all Al Gore's. Gore did carry all three states, but not nearly as dramatically as the coloring implied. Had less than half of one percent of the total West Coast vote shifted to Bush, two of the three Pacific coast states would have turned the networks' bright red. The Gore Coast was a graphics-driven exaggeration. The Pacific states were not nearly as solid for Gore as the colors looked. The same thing happened in the Great Lakes region. The Map painted all but two of the Great Lakes states as solidly for Gore, making the North Coast appear to be Gore country. But move 2 percent of the 20 million votes cast in the Great Lakes states and the entire region would have been red instead of two-thirds blue.

The Map has become the single most indelible metaphor in contemporary electoral politics. But this graphic metaphor exaggerates almost everything about those politics.

Self-Serving Arguments

Another factor here is political expediency. Leaders in both parties have their own reasons for pushing the polarization theme. Democrats know that since 2001 there has been a tilt toward the GOP. But calling that shift a minor realignment would be bad PR for Democrats. Better to call the phenomenon Polarization! That term characterizes Republican gains as somehow sinister, even dysfunctional.

Republicans have their own motives for embracing the myth of polarized politics. It's a good, all-purpose excuse for a party that holds the White House and controls the Congress but can't pass much of its legislative agenda. Why can't George Bush get his energy package adopted? Why can't the Republicans get 100 percent—instead of the actual 80 percent—of Bush's judicial appointments confirmed? It can't be the fault of the Republicans. So it must be the newly polarized political environment that's to blame.

Polarization is mostly an urban legend, imagined by the chattering classes of the metropolitan centers of politics and media.

For Democrats and Republicans, the new polarization is akin to the old partisanship. It's something both sides use to explain away almost anything and everything. Even the press has a self-serving motive for hyping polarization. Like partisanship, the specter of polarization gives the watchdog press a system-wide malfunction about which to bark.

Journalists aren't the only ones barking. For decades liberal academics actually argued in favor of polarization. Back then, political science labeled that prospect "responsible, coherent party politics." But now that we do have more coherent and consistent parties—even without violence or extremism—political scientists have joined the media in decrying the changes they once advocated.

This academic establishment balked when it became clear that coherence was increasing just as the Republicans were gaining ground. We suspect that if the Democrats were still the majority party and still controlled Congress and the presidency, the professoriate and the press would probably consider these changes to represent good, responsible government, not dreaded polarization.

Polarization is mostly an urban legend, imagined by the chattering classes of the metropolitan centers of politics and media. Still, as in any legend, there is truth here. But it isn't new and it isn't news. For decades white southerners have gravitated toward the Republicans. So the lion's share of conservatives are now in the conservative party. The abandoned Democrats have been left with almost all of the liberals. That's mainly how we became the "50-50" nation.

Unity Amid Division

If this transformation meant that neither blue voters nor red would cross the color line, then this might be cause for alarm. That hasn't happened. If this transformation led contemporary politics to the next level *down*—back into the streets or toward extremist movements—then one might be right to raise alarms about Polarization. But that hasn't happened either. . . .

This isn't a political picnic we're experiencing. . . . But what was a 19th-century maxim remains a 21st-century reality: Politics ain't beanbag.

More than 30 years ago, there was a popular slogan about the political crisis that was raging at the time: "We have met the enemy and he is us." Since 2001, we all know who the enemy is. And he isn't us. Americans recognize full well that their real enemy comes not from an American state that is either red or blue; he comes from a nation-state that has failed (like Afghanistan) or is failing (like Pakistan). How ironic that polarization theory should become received wisdom at a time when nationalistic fervor is greater than it has been for at least a decade.

Still, this isn't a political picnic we're experiencing in 2004. We can expect a nasty campaign and overheated rhetoric from both sides. But what was a 19th-century maxim remains a

21st-century reality: Politics ain't beanbag. Yet almost nothing the public has done since Campaign 2000 could be accurately described as antipodal or extremist, let alone radical.

How, then, best to describe the politics of the last few years? Each party has done about as well as the other in attracting voters, but the voters themselves have remained middle of the road. So we ought not to be too melodramatic in the labeling.

Kids might call this the politics of "Even Steven." Adults should prefer something more adult, but no more sensational. How about the era of Much Too Close To Call.

3

Voters Are Primarily Divided over Foreign Policy

Pew Research Center for the People and the Press

The Pew Research Center for the People and the Press is an independent research group that studies public opinion on politics and policy issues.

Polling shows that Republicans and Democrats are primarily divided by their opinions about national security. Republicans generally favor the use of military force, whereas Democrats overwhelmingly support diplomacy to maintain the country's security. In the past the parties were divided over a variety of issues, including religion, sexual issues, welfare, and business regulations, and pollsters had to ask a series of questions about these issues to predict whether a person was a Republican or a Democrat. Now pollsters can predict voters' political party by eliciting their views on one issue: the relative effectiveness of military force versus diplomacy.

Public attitudes on national security are now much more strongly associated with partisan affiliation than they were in the late 1990s. A comprehensive study of long-term public values finds that beliefs about national security are now twice as important as economic or social values in shaping a person's partisan identification. Five years ago, these national security values barely registered as a correlate of partisanship.

The survey of the public's values by the Pew Research Center for the People & the Press, conducted Dec. 1–16 [2004]

Pew Research Center for the People and the Press, "Politics and Values in a 51%–48% Nation: National Security More Linked with Partisan Affiliation," http://people-press.org, January 24, 2005.

among 2,000 adults, finds considerable evidence of the nation's political divisions. It also shows the public is attuned to the increasingly partisan environment—two-thirds (66%) believe the country is more politically divided than in the past, and roughly half say the people they know are more divided.

The war in Iraq is seen as the primary cause for the increasing divisiveness. The war has intensified partisan differences over long-term attitudes toward national security—notably, whether military strength, or good diplomacy, is the best way to ensure peace. On that measure and others, Republicans are more hawkish than in past values surveys, while Democrats have become more dovish. . . .

Security Divide Deepens

[The 2004] election underscored the stark divisions over the war in Iraq. The exit poll by the National Election Pool found that 79% of [Republican George W.] Bush voters said the war had improved U.S. security, while 88% of [Democrat John] Kerry voters said it had not.

Increasingly, that same divisiveness is seen in Pew's long term foreign policy and national security measures. Indeed, our values survey showed that, taken together, attitudes on the efficacy of force versus diplomacy, and on the obligation of Americans to fight for their country, are now by far the strongest predictors of whether a person is a Republican or a Democrat. These attitudes surpass opinions on every other subject—including attitudes toward homosexuality, religion and the role of government in helping the poor—in predicting partisanship.

Of course, differences over America's place in the world are not new. Indeed, it would be hard to argue that the political tensions over national security are any greater now than they were during the Vietnam or Korean Wars. Even in the 1990s, when national security largely receded as a public concern, there were substantial disagreements over the efficacy of military force and over Americans' obligation to fight for their country.

Attitudes on the efficacy of force versus diplomacy ... are now by far the strongest predictors of whether a person is a Republican or a Democrat.

What has changed since then is the extent to which attitudes toward national security influence partisan affiliation and voting decisions. During the 1990s, attitudes about government, welfare and business—as well as opinions concerning homosexuality—were most important in determining party affiliation, voting decisions, and presidential approval. But today, a single question—regarding the relative effectiveness of force versus diplomacy—is as powerful a predictor of party identification as the full set of values questions were in 1999.

Democratic Shift on Security

Significantly, the values study found little change in the public's overall views on basic foreign policy attitudes, even as Republicans and Democrats have grown further apart. A modest majority of all Americans (55%) said in December 2004 that good diplomacy, not military strength, is the best way to ensure peace. That was the same number who held that view in 1999 and virtually the same as in 1996 (53%).

However, an increasing number of Republicans subscribe to the view that military strength—rather than effective diplomacy—is the best way to ensure peace. The percentage endorsing diplomacy as the better option dropped from 46% in 1999 to 32% in 2004.

The movement among Democrats—in the opposite direction—has been just as dramatic. In the 1990s, roughly 60% of

Democrats expressed the view that good diplomacy was the best way to ensure peace; that number rose to 76% in 2004.

A similar pattern is evident in views on the obligation to fight for the country, whether it is right or wrong.

As in the 1990s, the public remained split on this measure—46% thought a person should fight, whether the country is right or wrong, while an identical number said it is acceptable for someone to decline to fight in a war they see as morally wrong.

Since 1999, an increasing number of Republicans express the view that a person has an obligation to fight, while Democrats have moved in the opposite direction. By 66% to 27%, Republicans said that people should fight for the country, right or wrong; Democrats, by a comparable margin said it is acceptable to refuse to fight in a war that one sees as morally wrong.

Election Intensifies Differences

Pew first found evidence of a growing political gap in national security values . . . in our major survey on the American political landscape in November 2003. If anything, the 2004 election appears to have intensified these differences.

Roughly two-thirds of Bush voters said that using overwhelming force is the best way to defeat global terrorism. An even larger percentage of Kerry voters said that relying too much on military force creates hatred that leads to more terrorism.

Bush and Kerry voters also expressed starkly different views about the U.S. role in world affairs. While a majority of Bush voters endorsed an activist foreign policy, just as many Kerry voters instead agreed with the statement: "We should pay less attention to problems overseas and concentrate on problems here at home."

4

Voters Are Primarily Divided over Moral Values

Brad Carson

Brad Carson is a former Democratic congressman from Oklahoma.

A major cause of the political divide is a growing split over moral values in America. Millions of voters care passionately about moral and cultural issues and will only vote for candidates who share their values. Moreover, the divide over moral values is not merely about issues such as abortion or gay marriage. It is part of a deeper philosophical split over nationalism versus globalization, individualism versus community, and old-fashioned values like honor versus modern tolerance.

I don't remember when I first realized that my [2004] campaign for United States Senate was in trouble. But one moment stands out. I was in Sallisaw, Oklahoma, home of the annual Grapes of Wrath Festival, in which locals celebrate John Steinbeck's fictional Joad family [of Steinbeck's 1939 novel *The Grapes of Wrath*] and their mythical journey from eastern Oklahoma to California. It was a Sunday morning, one week before the third anniversary of the September 11 [2001] terrorist attacks, and I had been invited by the pastor of a local Baptist church to discuss the topic: "How Would Jesus Vote?" Both my opponent in the Senate race, [Republican] Tom Coburn, and I had been invited to what was more or less an interview before the pastor's congregation. I would go first, then Coburn would speak the following Sunday, and a right-wing talk-radio host—no friend of mine, to be sure—would conclude the three-week inquiry into how Jesus would want us to cast our ballots.

Now, I must confess: My own view is that Jesus would probably not vote at all, given the organized corruption that passes for modern American politics. But the idea that Christ Himself might sit out the 2004 election was apparently not under consideration, so I accepted the invitation—much to the pastor's avowed surprise. As an active Baptist who grew up in the Baptist church, I had no illusions that most of my co-religionists were ardent Democrats, but I rarely turned down any chance to make the case for my own candidacy and that of my fellow party members. After all, wasn't Daniel blessed for braving the lion's den?

The culture war is real, and it is a conflict not merely about some particular policy or legislative item, but about modernity itself.

Voting Righteously

As I arrived at the church, my wife and I were given the church bulletin, which outlined the weekly selection of hymns and Bible readings. On the back of the bulletin, atop the blank space reserved for copious note-taking during the sermon, was the heading: "WWJV? PRO-LIFE OR PRO-DEATH?" (I favored the partial-birth abortion ban but opposed overturning *Roe* v. *Wade* [the Supreme Court decision that declared abortion a Constitutional right].) In the sanctuary, a 20-by-20-foot depiction of a fetus looked down upon the assembled throng from a projection screen. Superimposed upon the unsettling image—which morphed to show the fetus in various stages of gestation—was fact after fact about abortions in America.

After the morning rituals, the pastor called me to the stage, and we engaged in a lengthy discussion about abortion, homosexuality, "liberal judges," and other controversial matters. After leaving the stage, I rejoined the congregation, and the pastor launched into an attack on the "pro-choice terrorists," who were, to his mind, far more dangerous than Al Qaeda. Yes, he acknowledged, thousands had died on September 11, but abortion was killing millions and millions. This was a holocaust, he continued, and we must all vote righteously. *Vote righteously!* In 13 months of campaigning across the vast state of Oklahoma, I must have seen or heard this phrase a thousand times, often on the marquees of churches, where, outside of election season, one finds only clever and uplifting biblical bromides. But it was not until that September Sunday in Sallisaw, one of the most Democratic towns in Oklahoma, that I first understood that the seemingly innocuous phrase "vote righteously" was the slogan not of a few politicized churches, but the *cri de coeur* ["cry of the heart"] of millions—millions who fervently believe that their most deeply held values are under assault and who further see this assault as at least tolerated by the Democratic Party, if not actually led by it.

The Culture War Is Real

As a defeated Senate candidate in the most red of red states, many people have asked me for insights into the Democratic Party's failure to connect with culturally conservative voters. Much has already been written on this topic, and scholars will add more. But I do know this: The culture war is real, and it is a conflict not merely about some particular policy or legislative item, but about modernity itself. Banning gay marriage or abortion would not be sufficient to heal the cultural gulf that exists in this nation. The culture war is about matters more fundamental still: whether nationality is, in a globalized world, a random fact of no more significance than what hospital one was born in or whether it is the source of identity and even political legitimacy; whether one's self is a matter of choice or whether it is predetermined, before birth, by the cultural membership of one's family; whether an individual is just that—a free-floating atom—or whether the individual is part of a long chain that both predates and continues long after any particular person; whether concepts like honor and shame, which seem so quaint, are still relevant in a world that values only "tolerance." These are questions not for politicians but for philosophers, and, in the end, it is the failure of liberal philosophy that we saw on November 2 [2004, when Republican George W. Bush defeated Democrat John Kerry].

The voters aren't deluded or uneducated. They simply reject the notion that material concerns are more real than spiritual or cultural ones.

For the vast majority of Oklahomans—and, I would suspect, voters in other red states—these transcendent cultural concerns are more important than universal health care or raising the minimum wage or preserving farm subsidies. . . . The voters aren't deluded or uneducated. They simply reject the notion that material concerns are more real than spiritual or cultural ones. The political left has always had a hard time understanding this, preferring to believe that the masses are enthralled by a "false consciousness" or Fox News or whatever today's excuse might be. But the truth is quite simple: Most voters in a state like Oklahoma—and I venture to say most other Southern and Midwestern states—reject the general direction of American culture and celebrate the political party that promises to reform or revise it.

That is what [Supreme Court Justice] Antonin Scalia famously called the *Kulturkampf* ["culture war"]. And there can be no doubt either that this is a fundamental dynamic in American politics or on which side of this conflict the electorate rests. [On the 2004 Election Day], I ran 7 percent ahead of [Democratic presidential candidate] John Kerry, and my opponent ran a full 13 percent behind President Bush. In most states, this would have been more than sufficient to ensure my victory. But not in Oklahoma. At least not [in 2004]. And, while the defeat was all my own, the failure was of the party to which I swear allegiance, which uncritically embraces a modernity that so many others reject.

5

The Moral Values Divide Is Exaggerated

Dick Meyer

Dick Meyer is the editorial director of CBSNews.com.

The idea that voters are sharply divided according to their beliefs about moral issues is based on false evidence and bad logic. Much-cited polls showing "moral values" as voters' top concern are flawed. The percentage of voters citing "moral values" or "family values" as their number one concern has remained relatively constant over the years, yet Democrats won two presidential elections in the 1990s. This record shows that the right Democratic candidate can win over religious voters without changing the Democratic party's fundamental beliefs.

L et's try to snuff [the 2004] election's new Big Theory before it becomes Conventional Wisdom, although it's probably too late.

The subject matter is "moral values." The theory is this: [Democratic candidate John] Kerry lost because he was very unpopular with people who believe moral values are the most important issues. This group of values voters is growing and Democrats are doomed until they can win them over.

The evidence comes from one exit poll question: Which issue mattered most in deciding how you voted for president? Here are the results:

	KERRY	BUSH
Moral Values (22%)	18%	80%
Economy/Jobs (20%)	80%	18%
Terrorism (19%)	14%	86%
Iraq (15%)	73%	26%
Health Care (8%)	77%	23%
Taxes (5%)	43%	57%
Education (4%)	73%	26%

Analysts and commentators have been stunned that moral issues would trump the other biggies. From this single result, where moral values trounced economy/jobs by a whole two percentage points, both gloaters and mourners have extrapolated a fatal flaw in the Democratic Party and all it encompasses. An industry of values voter literature has mushroomed in just the few days since the election. It's misguided.

While the nexus of issues boiled into the words "moral values" certainly were a big factor in this election, it's being exaggerated partly because of the oddities of the poll itself and partly because the Big Theory conforms with what Republican strategists want you to believe.

Polling Flaws

First, the poll: If the poll had been worded or constructed only slightly differently, moral values would not have been the top issue. We're building a worldview out of a small, odd vista.

If, for example, one of the issues on the list was a combined "terrorism and Iraq," it would have been the top concern of 34 percent of the electorate and nobody would be talking about moral values.

If "taxes, jobs and the economy" was on the list as one item instead of two, it would have been the topper at 25 percent.

If, say, abortion rights, gay marriage and moral values were all on the list separately, the numbers would be very different.

Who knows what the exit poll would have found if "truth in government" were an option. Polls are fickle.

As for the notion that the legion of values voters is exploding, I don't see it.

In 2000, exit poll victims were not given moral values as an option on their "most important issues" menu (partly because it would have just been seen as a question about [President] Bill [Clinton] and Monica [Lewinsky, the intern with whom he had an affair]). So we don't really know whether the slice of the electorate concerned with such things has grown in Bush's term, as is purported.

Democrats will never be the favorite party of people who put gay marriage and other "moral values" at the top of their list.

We do know that in a similar question from the 1996, "family values" was the top concern of 17 percent (just behind the winner, "health of the economy"), and that group went for [Republican] Bob Dole over [Democrat] Bill Clinton. So, the 17 percent whose top worry was family values and whose choice was Republican turned into 22 percent worried about moral values in 2004. A factor in this election? Sure. But not a hurricane; perhaps a tropical depression.

If you want to see a polling hurricane, consider that "terrorism" has never been any kind of concern before. That's a sea change. No foreign policy or national security has gotten into the top four issues in the last three elections [1992, 1996, and 2000]. [In 2004], as we saw, terror and Iraq were the prime issues for more than a third of the voters.

Defining Moral Values

Next problem: what are these moral values? . . .

Now, we all have a sense of what is meant by moral values in [the 2004] election: gay marriage, stem cell research, late-term abortion, prayer in school and several other similar issues. What it really refers to is being *against* gay marriage, stem cell research and late-term abortion. Being adamantly *for* stem cell research would exclude you from being part of the moral values crowd.

Moral values, as a phrase on an exit poll, is a Rorschach Test; to a great degree, the question is like asking, "What is most important to you—jobs, terrorism, health care, education, or the issue that is really the most important issue to you." It's tautological.

And in the code of politics and rhetoric, the phrase "moral values" really now just refers to a set of Bush's positions. So the exit poll question is even dumber; of course people who think moral values are most important will go for Bush.

For these reasons, the exit poll question that is changing the world really doesn't tell us very much. The political conclusions people are drawing from this narrow finding are obviously pretty flimsy.

Other Political Divisions

For instance, since it is now an accepted crisis for the Democrats that the values voters who were 22 percent of the electorate went for the Republican by an 80-18 margin, it must follow that it's a crisis for Republicans that the 20 percent who care most about the economy and jobs went 80-18 for the Democrat.

Is it a crisis for the Republicans that the huge, 45 percent slice of the electorate that describes itself as moderate went for Kerry 54-45?

Is it a crisis for the Republicans first time voters went 53-46 for Kerry? Doesn't that make an ominous sign for the future?

It's argued that the Democrats are in hot water because the rural voters who made up 16 percent of the electorate went 59-40 for Bush. Is it a crisis for the Republicans that the 13 percent that live in big cities went 60-39 for Kerry?

The voting behavior of Americans does divvy up into some pretty stark and feuding neighborhoods. Rural voters and heavy church-goers vote Republican. City people and church-avoiders vote Democratic. These cleavages have persisted in several elections.

Those divides may be a crisis for the country; they may describe a culture war, at least for the politically active. It is not an inherent crisis for Democrats alone. And the inability to win the allegiance of people who care most about the amorphous thing currently called moral values is not at the top of the Democrats' problems. Republicans, however, want people to believe that the Democrats are simply categorically different than the good people who care about moral things.

Democrats' Problems

After debunking this theory du jour with such vitriol, permit me the Kerryesque weakness of making a few qualifiers.

I do think many active Democrats—appointees, consultants, volunteers, and partisans—have a deep disrespect for religious people, old-fashioned people and country people. It's palpable and it's deplorable and Democrats deny it. And it means that party activists and related groups bring to forum issues that are in fact unpopular, like support for gay marriage.

I also think many active Republicans are just as snotty; they just pretend better.

And I think many religious people, old-fashioned people and country people have a profound disrespect for "liberals" and people they disagree with and people who aren't like them. But that is sort of reverse snobbery so it's okay.

Democratic politicians—at least the ones who score big in national politics—have a fundamental conflict; they always purport to represent people who aren't very much like them;

they are rich and white and pedigreed and claim to represent the poor or the working class or gays or minorities. Republicans don't have that problem; they tend to represent themselves and their kind.

The [Democrats'] so-called values voters' crisis can be solved by the right candidate. It's not brain surgery.

This Democratic impulse may be noble and right, but it's hard to pull off. Bill Clinton could do it (though it did his party little lasting good). But when an Al Gore or a John Kerry does it, it looks inauthentic and it makes people uncomfortable. It makes people feel like they don't share their moral values. (Indeed, Kerry embodied icons of being a values voter's worst nightmare—liberal, from Massachusetts, married to a rich, foreign, billionaire heiress.)

Democrats will never be the favorite party of people who put gay marriage and other "moral values" at the top of their list. And if the Democrats' response to the moral values concept is a sanctimonious "well, starting a war and killing innocent Iraqis isn't a moral value" then they have a crisis.

But many Democrats have done and will do a better job of speaking to a far bigger group than values voters—religious people and church-goers who balance many issues in a complicated way and who are not hardcore partisans.

[2004's] failure is not intrinsic to what the Democratic Party is or what it might stand for. Family values were a very big deal 20 years ago in the reign of Ronald Reagan. (One of the more visible advocates was Democrat Tipper Gore.) Yet Democrat Bill Clinton then won two terms. The so-called values voters' crisis can be solved by the right candidate. It's not brain surgery.

The Democrats' inability to find such candidates and then let them lead, however, appears to be a very difficult condition to cure.

6

The Political Divide Makes Honest Policy Debate More Difficult

David Brooks

David Brooks was an editor and columnist for the Wall Street Journal *and the* Weekly Standard *and has been an op-ed columnist for the* New York Times *since 2003. He is the author of several books, including* Bobos in Paradise: The New Upper Class and How They Got There *and* On Paradise Drive: How We Live Now (And Always Have) in the Future Tense.

The political divide is harmful to America because intense partisanship causes people to have more loyalty to their political "team" than to the country, or even to the truth. In this atmosphere, debate becomes more of a contest to score points for one's team than about honestly discussing solutions to problems. This partisan attitude even extends to voters' views of reality: rather than using facts and logic to choose a political philosophy, voters choose a political philosophy and then shape their views of reality to fit their politics. Middle ground for consensus exists on many social and political issues, but it is difficult to see because of this extreme partisanship.

A running argument I have been having with members of the [George W.] Bush administration is revelatory of how they think about discourse and democracy. The first column I

David Brooks, "A Polarized America," *Hedgehog Review*, volume 6, issue 3, Fall 2004. Based on the transcript of the Labrosse-Levinson Lecture given by Brooks at the University of Virginia, October 20, 2004.

wrote for *The New York Times* ... began something like this: "People in the Bush administration will never admit a mistake, but they do change the way they effect policy." I got a call the next day from a friend in the administration to talk about why they never admit a mistake. He described a comment, made experimentally, admitting a mistake. He and many in the administration had taken a trip to Baghdad [Iraq] shortly after the ground war ended [in 2003]. When they came back, [Deputy Secretary of Defense] Paul Wolfowitz said publicly, "We made five mistakes so far in this war," and listed them. The headlines the next day were, "Wolfowitz: We Were Stupid" and other negative sound bites.

My friend's point was that Washington D.C. is a not a town in which you can have a give-and-take conversation on issues. The town is so polarized that admitting a mistake gives your opponents a chance to leap on you and then spend the next two weeks talking about your admitted mistake. He said, "We [in the Bush administration] have found ourselves surrounded by Democrats who, when we bring them into the White House, go out on the White House lawn and trash it. The press is only interested in taking us down—not only because they may ideologically differ, but because it is their job to take down administrations." His argument was that, in this polarized age, any administration has to have a communications strategy. And the communications strategy that [the Bush] administration came up with was based on the idea that you never make concessions. You may have journalists and public intellectuals who want to know how you are making decisions, who want to see you weigh the pros and cons, who want to engage in an argument with you, but you strategically choose never to take part in that argument. You never let them see you make a decision. You never publicly deliberate because the system is so broken, with such strong backlash, that you cannot afford to reveal such information.

The "Zone of Trust"

This consciously made decision means that, even for those of us who cover the administration closely, you never really see the inside. This administration has built what you might call a "zone of trust." There are certain people within that zone, who are there when the decisions and deliberations are undertaken, but from outside this zone, you see that decisions are made and then see that changes to those decisions are made. . . .

[The Bush] administration knew that a zone of trust would make the press very hostile—which has happened—but they felt the upsides were more than compensated for. First, they thought opening up would just give their political opponents ammunition. Second, they had seen what had happened to the first [George H.W.] Bush administration [from 1989 to 1993], which was riven by leaks and people exposing internal arguments to the media. Third, they wanted team unity. They wanted to have a cohesive group of people who would always stick together, through thick and thin. Fourth, setting up the President this way projected a resoluteness to the country. It communicated that he was not going to concede to elite opinion. They thought this was, in the long run, a winning political strategy. Fifth, the President would not be seen as a creature of Washington, obsessed with the editorial pages of *The New York Times*, *The Washington Post*, or the salons of Georgetown. Finally, they thought people within the zone of trust would speak more freely, knowing that what they said would not be leaked.

In this world, loyalty to one's teammates is more important than loyalty to the truth.

I would argue against this way of thinking about the zone of trust. I think elite opinion actually matters, and it is very hard to govern if the elite opinion is against you. By kissing it all off, per se, they have made life immeasurably more difficult for themselves. They have driven away potential allies, including moderate Democrats who wanted to work with the administration on a whole range of issues. For example, there were about ten Senate Democrats, including Joe Biden, Evan Bayh, Joe Lieberman, and Hillary Clinton, who wanted to go in and be part of the team. They felt they had something to offer. What the Bush administration did was exaggerate the extent to which you could not have a serious debate about policy in Washington, and it became a self-fulfilling prophecy. If you drive people out, you will have a polarized situation in Washington. You can learn something by bringing in people who are not within your zone. [Dissident Republican senator] Chuck Hagel and Joe Biden would have had things to say about post-war Iraq that were quietly said within the administration, but maybe not with as much force as these more public voices would have said them. There is some virtue in having conversation.

Never Admit a Mistake

Unfortunately, I think my opponents in this disagreement are right politically: the nature of Washington politics is such that if you want to thrive politically, you must never admit a mistake. If you poll both Democratic and Republican consultants, they will agree on this point. At an awkward press conference, Bush was asked, "Have you ever made a mistake?" And he replied, "I can't think of one at the moment." I was with a bunch of Democratic and Republican consultants, who said that it was a painful moment, but agreed that he did the right thing. If you admit a mistake, they argued, then you are opening yourself up.

I got a little taste of what this was like in April and May of 2004 when I wrote a series of six columns in *The New York Times* on mistakes I had made in thinking about the war in Iraq. What I found was that my friends in the conservative community hated me and thought I was a turncoat. The people to whom I was making some concessions grew more hostile to me than ever. I got no credit for trying to think through things. Admitting mistakes was seen not only as a sign that I was wrong, but also as a sign that I was a coward and weak. Maybe there is something right in the stonewall strategy.

In our polarized political world, the debate we are having is not a disagreement about a certain set of issues: we are having a disagreement about what reality is.

Team Spirit in Politics

However, in terms of governance and in terms of winning over and trying to expand your majority, I think the administration made a mistake. The decision to create a zone of trust was a mistake because it increased the dominant factor of life in Washington, which is not ideology, but team spirit. People who are Republicans are part of the Republican team. People who are Democrats are part of the Democratic team. People who are in the administration are part of the administration team. In this world, loyalty to one's teammates is more important than loyalty to the truth. As we think about discourse and democracy, it is important to remind ourselves that it is not as if there used to be a golden age of honesty and good debate and open exchange, and now there is a decline. No. In reality, anyone in public life has two competing value systems. There is loyalty to the truth, saying what you believe, and loyalty to your calling; and then there is loyalty to your brethren and to your party. If you want to get anything done in public life, you have to have a team, and you have to say things that help the team. Often, in fact almost always, if team playing means shading the truth, one shades the truth in order to help the team.

You can be like Chuck Hagel has been over the past year and say what you really think about Iraq—and Chuck Hagel has said a lot of smart things—but you will not be allowed to be a major team player, just as Chuck Hagel has been let go by the Republican party. You will not help pass an agenda. You will be a lone wolf on the talk shows. Even if most senators agree with you, they will decide it is a better form of public service to do what benefits the team. This is why members of the administration, on both the left and the right, do not tell the truth. This is why they say things that they know are dishonest and untrue, as both presidential candidates did in the [2004] election campaigns. They knew what they were doing. They are not stupid, but they were serving a cause that they thought was more important. They thought that dodging the truth would help the team in the long run, even though they knew it was dirty. Team loyalty and duty to the public creates a powerful tension that affects the form of discourse. People serve their teams.

In our polarized political world, the debate we are having is not a disagreement about a certain set of issues: we are having a disagreement about what reality is. The two different parties describe two different realities. You do not choose who has the best policies; you choose the best reality, the reality that seems truer to you. You turn on the television, and you are not watching a debate; you are watching someone vindicate your side, your team. There are a couple of "Crossfire" representatives on your team; there are a couple members from the other side. You feel good if your team does well, and you get mad if your team lets you down. As we think about public discourse, it is important to grapple with what team competition is about.

What are we fighting about? [In 1998] the country essentially went into parity in politics. The Republicans and the Democrats essentially stood tied at 49 to 49 percent. In 2000, we stayed at parity. Both parties were tied in this bitter feud. Since then we've had the war on terror, the 9/11 attack, the collapse of the dot-coms, a recession, and corporate scandals. We've had millions of people dying, millions of people moving every year, and an influx of tens of millions of immigrants. Everything has changed—except for the political divide. It's still 49/49, and if you look at the states that are closely divided, their divisions are the same. The demographic groups are the same. There is something very stable at the heart of this divide. What is this about?

The Sources of the Divide

If you look at the two parties, there are differences in geography and in culture, with differing character and personalities. There are differences in foreign and domestic policy. Somehow two guys with incredibly similar family trees—[John] Kerry's family came over soon after the Mayflower, and Bush's family on the boat right after that—represent two sides of this debate. Many rivers feed into this polarization.

One of them, for example, is education. You would think that as the country became better educated, it would also become more flexible. You would have more independent thinkers. You would have people switching parties back and forth, listening to candidates debating the issues. But the fact is that the more educated the electorate gets, the more polarized it gets, with less ticket switching. In 1960, only four percent of registered voters had college degrees. Now, the percentage is up around 30, 40, 50 percent, depending on who you ask. The more educated a voter is, the less likely that voter is to switch parties. Highly educated voters vote for the same party again and again and again. They don't switch sides because they ask themselves this question: Am I liberal or am I conservative? And once they give themselves an ideological label, it is unlikely they are going to switch.

Another river feeding into our polarization is media segmentation. We can all find media outlets that we agree with
and that reinforce our views. There is a story that somebody
at Fox News told me, which we in the journalism business say
is too good to check out, but I will relate it, because I think it
says something important. Some Fox viewers would wake up
at six in the morning, turn on Fox, and watch Fox all day,
turning off their sets at midnight. When these people turned
off their sets, they found that the translucent logo at the bot-
tom of the screen had burned into their television because the
logo position never changed. So Fox found that they had to
move their logo across the screen. A simple story, perhaps untrue, but symbolic of a certain sort of segmentation. People
choose a single news source, which in effect cancels out different views. Instead, one is told, "you're right, you're right,
you're right," and challenging views disappear. One's view
naturally becomes polarized.

---

*People filter reality through their partisan labels. They
choose the reality that makes them feel the best.*

Another way we are segmenting is geographically. We're all
familiar with the red and blue America map from the 2000
election. I call it the global warming map because if the polar
ice caps melt and the coasts and the Mississippi Valley flood,
the Democratic Party will be wiped off the face of the earth.
Over time this map is getting more and more pronounced.
The number of counties in this country with a landslide majority has doubled in a generation. People are really good at
finding people like themselves. . . .

These geographic splits are also related to income. In Mur-
freesboro, Tennessee, for example, it used to be that there was
a local banker who was the richest person in town. After him,
there were some executives, and then there were some farm-
ers, store owners, and mill workers. That bank is now head-

quartered in Charlotte, North Carolina. The executives all live at some corporate headquarters in New York, so there are no rich people left in that town. Demographically and politically, it has become segmented. . . .

Partisan Views of Reality

I alluded to another division when I talked about team spirit, which is partisanship. When you identify yourself as a Republican or a Democrat, that doesn't only give you a way to register. It shapes the way you see the world. People filter reality through their partisan labels. They choose the reality that makes them feel the best. For example, at the end of the Reagan terms, Republicans and Democrats were asked: Did inflation decline during [Republican] Ronald Reagan's presidency? In reality, it did decline, from 11 to 3 percent, but 60 percent of Democrats said it went up under Reagan. They were wrong, but they chose the reality that reflected what they thought of the Reagan administration. After the Clinton years, people were again asked about certain economic indicators and whether they rose or fell. This time it was Republicans' turn to be wrong.

Being a Republican or a Democrat is really important to people. They choose their reality and their belief system on the basis of their partisan affiliation. Most people inherit their partisan affiliation, or they form it early in adulthood by figuring out which party is most affiliated with people like them. Once they decide they are Republican, they become interested in the marketplace of capitalism. Once they decide they are Democratic, they become interested in equality and social justice. Partisan affiliation, in many cases, precedes a belief system—not the other way around. Another thing that deeply divides us—and it goes to one of the reasons we have so much trouble talking to each other—is that in this country we are debating leadership; we are debating about what qualities a leader should have. It has been said that all societies have two aristocracies: an aristocracy of money and an aristocracy of mind. The aristocracy of money is filled with people who build things and make money. The aristocracy of mind is filled with people who use their minds to produce ideas and concepts. Different cultures exist between managers and professionals, and they vote differently. Professionals are people like doctors, lawyers, professors, and journalists who tend to vote more Democratic. Managers are people like corporate executives who tend to vote more Republican. This division shows up in donations. If you look at what categories of people give to Republicans and to Democrats, it is amazing how important career is in who people are likely to support financially. CEOs, for example, give to Republicans in a ratio of 5-to-1; that is, for every one CEO who donates money to the Democrats, there are five who donate money to the Republicans, which is not surprising. Accountants and bankers give primarily to Republicans. All the "aristocracy of money" gives to Republicans. On the other hand, lawyers give to Democrats by a ratio of 3-to-1. Actors gave to the Gore campaign by a ratio of 18-to-1; journalists by a ratio of 93-to-1; librarians by a ratio of 223-to-1. . . . The single biggest group of donors to the Kerry campaign was the employees of the University of California. The second single biggest group was the employees of Harvard University. In other words, employees of academic institutions were giving more to Democrats than employees of Goldman Sachs [a financial services corporation] and CitiBank.

Partisan affiliation, in many cases, precedes a belief system—not the other way around.

The argument is not so much over ideology, though that is one element. It is not only about geography, or partisanship, or lifestyle. It is also about what sort of people should run the country. What values are important in a President?

Some people who might be on the professional side of this argument take a look at George Bush and think he is exactly the wrong sort of person to run the country. Some people on the corporate side take a look at the virtues he possesses and say he is exactly the right sort of person to run the country. Two groups of Americans segmented off in various ways take a look at the same individual, with radically different reactions to him. . . .

Unified, Yet Polarized

What I have tried to describe here is a Washington that is riven; any administration has to figure out how to govern in this scene of polarization. How do we govern in an age in which people do not agree on the same reality? How do we govern in an age in which large degrees of hostility are present on television, in the press and the Senate, and in private life? The Bush administration made a rational political decision to try not to engage this polarization, and they increased the polarization. It was not a politically foolish decision. They went in saying they were going to try to work across party lines, but when the pressures came, team loyalty trumped loyalty to the truth.

How do we govern in an age in which people do not agree on the same reality?

Policy differences are not a part of the problem. We have always had policy differences. If you poll people and if you get experts together, you come to one inexplicable conclusion: that on most issues, even on issues like abortion, health insurance, and education, it is very possible to find middle ground. Issues don't explain the partisan divide; rather, something has invaded the psychology and social structure of our country. This mysterious but permanent rift in the body politic looks as stable and as divisive and as permanent today, for all we have been through in the past four years, as it did four years ago, suggesting that this is a permanent state of affairs.

But we have to remind ourselves that Americans are all tremendously alike. If you take people in red or blue America, people in the Bush administration or people who worked with Kerry, if you look at the way they actually live, Americans across red and blue have similar divorce rates, similar statistics of sexual activity, similar frequencies in moving and job change, education, even television watching. To some extent, Americans are a tremendously unified people—unified, yet polarized.

7

The Current Political Divide Is Beneficial

Jonah Goldberg

Jonah Goldberg is a syndicated columnist and editor-at-large of National Review Online, a conservative Web site.

Political division of some sort is an unavoidable part of human nature. In the past, people primarily divided themselves according to race, class, religion, and/or ethnicity. However, since the 1950s people have been dividing themselves according to political persuasion and ideology instead. This sort of division by political ideology is healthier for American society than division by race or class.

Americans are becoming more tolerant of everybody, except the people they disagree with.

I have no idea if this is an interesting, obvious, or idiotic observation to most people. But I find it pretty interesting. And since I control the vertical and I control the horizontal—as they say in *Outer Limits*—I'm going to discuss it for a moment.

There's been a lot of talk lately—much of it whiny—about "polarization" in American politics. Wahhh: [Liberal filmmaker] Michael Moore is hellspawn. Or: Wahhh: Michael Moore is a secular prophet and the Pharisees of the ruling class are crucifying him.

Others have complained that liberals and conservatives don't read the same books anymore so they can't even agree on common facts for reasonable disagreements (which would explain the Hellspawn v. Prophet thing).

Education Increases Polarization

David Brooks has been pounding the keyboard until his fingers run bloody on the issue lately. And he raises several interesting observations and facts in the process. For example, for all the self-congratulatory English-major talk about how education breeds independent thinking and clear-eyed appreciation for the nuances of reality. . . . Oh wait, English major talk sounds like this: "Do you want foam on that half-caf latte?" Political-science majors are more likely to spew all that stuff about the enlightenment and independent thinking that comes with education.

Anyway, whoever says that stuff is wrong. The fact is that the more educated you are, the more partisan and ideological you are likely to be. High-school graduates are more likely to vote across party lines than college grads. And education does not track only with becoming more liberal. If you're a conservative with a college education you become more conservative. If you're a liberal, ditto. Indeed, college-educated liberals tend to become "professionals" while college-educated conservatives become "managers." Brooks breaks all that stuff down even more, but I think you get the point. Though maybe the guy running the espresso machine can't hear me.

Political Self-Segregation

Anyway, in his book, *On Paradise Drive*, Brooks compiles a massive amount of evidence that Americans are self-segregating ideologically and politically—by county, by school, by state, by church, etc. An example he doesn't use, but which comes immediately to mind, are *National Review* cruises. As many of you no doubt know, *NR* has been a pioneer in the practice of conducting cruises for ideologically simpatico and faithful readers. They really are quite a lot of fun. But part of the logic is that while people want to go on cruises, they don't necessarily want to go on cruises with other people who want to go on cruises. I remember talking to one very impressive, and very conservative, retired judge on an *NR* cruise. He told me how he'd gone on a regular cruise and got stuck with a convention from a teachers' union or something. Everywhere he went, every dinner table, every game of blackjack was intruded upon by the sound of people saying things he thought were crazy. That's no vacation. So on the *NR* cruises, people of like—though certainly not of identical—political views get to attend some fun conferences and panels, but they also know they can have a pleasant dinner conversation. This isn't a plug for *NR* cruises. . . . But it is interesting how everybody uses the *NR* model now—or tries to. *The Nation, The New Republic, The Weekly Standard*, the NRA [National Rifle Association], *Salon*, the Heritage Foundation, etc.

The fact is that the more educated you are, the more partisan and ideological you are likely to be.

Anyway, David Brooks thinks this sort of polarization and self-segregation is bad. Moreover, he's been taking what I think is something of an unfair shellacking from various liberal writers. In a sense he's becoming the Rodney King of American conservatives. No matter how severe the beating he receives, he continues to say "Why can't we all just get along?"

Well, I have no intention of joining the beat down; I like and respect the guy too much. And, I agree that there are definitely some serious drawbacks to the polarization of the national discourse. Though, truth be told, I despise phrases like "national discourse" or "social dialogue" precisely because they tend to be used by liberals who believe "increasing dialogue" means in fact "educating the Huns to agree with us."

But, as Bob Dole would say, whatever.

The Benefits of Polarization

There's also a very good side to all of this polarization. Critics of identity politics—and I am most certainly one of them—tend to focus almost exclusively on the separations, divides, clashes and chasms such politics create between groups. Blacks vs. whites, rich vs. poor, South vs. North, Springfieldians vs. Shelbyvillians, and so on. What they rarely look at is the unity such "identitarian" movements create. This was, after all, one of the central dynamics of fascism—it was a cross-class movement of national unity. Rich and poor alike joined hands in their unity under the swastika. And Communism, no less a reactionary force than fascism (and often more of one), caused ethnic Ukrainians, Tartars, Uzbeks, Russians et al. to lay down their ethnic differences in their common struggle against the ruling classes.

Manifestations of ethnic intolerance today tend to decrease in proportion as ideological intolerance increases. In sharp contrast, both bigotries used to increase together.

America is hardly immune to these laws of social attraction and repulsion. Take McCarthyism. Liberals love to point out the Manichean worldview behind McCarthyism. How it created enemies within. How Tail-gunner Joe's [Joseph McCarthy, Republican senator from Wisconsin from 1947 to 1957] followers went after anybody—Jews, blacks, whites, Catholics, Protestants, Republicans, Democrats—anybody who he believed to be a Commie or ComSymp [Communist or Communist sympathizer]. Without getting into that whole argument again, let's just say fair enough. But, one thing left out of this analysis is how the McCarthyites *didn't* go after Jews, blacks, whites, Catholics, etc., who *agreed* with McCarthy about the Red menace. This may be an obvious fact of logic but it's actually much more revealing than it seems.

"Manifestations of ethnic intolerance today tend to decrease in proportion as ideological intolerance increases. In sharp contrast, both bigotries used to increase together," wrote Peter Viereck in 1955. What Viereck noticed was that radical "right-wing" anti-Communist groups were reaching out to blacks and Jews (those quotation marks around "right-wing" are necessary for reasons we'll get into another day). The same thing, of course, had already been taking place on the other side since Communists believe in class-loyalty and all that gibberish. In other words, pro-Communists and anti-Communists alike welcomed rich and poor, Jew and gentile, black and white into their respective ranks—so long as the applicant in question agreed on the "big issue."

Liberals still talk about the 1960s as if all real Americans were sitting around, holding hands, and singing "Kumbaya.". . . How many misty-eyed stories have we heard about how blacks and whites, Jews and Christians, all marched together for peace and love and whatnot? What they always leave out is that there were often whites, blacks, Christians, and Jews on the other side of the pickets who disagreed with them. In others words, ideological causes breed unity and disunity at the same time.

Transtolerance

Viereck called this dynamic "transtolerance," a terrible word that perfectly describes what is happening in America today. For example, there is no more philo-Semitic group in America than evangelical Christians. Indeed, they love observant Jews more than most Jews do. Why? Because the Right side of the culture war wants "traditionalists" of all stripes in its corner. Similarly, the American Right loves blacks—right-wing blacks that is. The Right hasn't caught up with the Left yet, where the "open-mindedness" of liberals causes their brains to fall out for any member of the Coalition of the Oppressed. But conservatives are certainly moving in that direction.

> *The Left doesn't really believe in class-warfare; it merely*
> *believes in class warfare against the rich folks who dis-*
> *agree with them.*

We see this in the ghettoized communities Brooks is so adept at chronicling. I sincerely doubt there are very many affluent "red state" counties in America that wouldn't love to have a socially conservative black stockbroker move into their community. I'm sure there are some racist country clubs and the like still around, but generally I would bet that most country clubs would leap at the opportunity to snap up a black or Jewish or Asian cardiologist. Why? Because conservatives very much believe—and want the world to know—that their views are principled, not prejudiced. Meanwhile, the Left has been reaching out to folks like George Soros, Arianna Huffington, and Teresa Heinz [all millionaires who support Democratic causes] who are, essentially class-traitors in Marxist thought. The Left doesn't really believe in class-warfare; it merely believes in class warfare against the rich folks who disagree with them.

As Viereck noticed, we have something new in American history: Ideological movements used to reinforce racial, ethnic, or class bigotries. For the last 50 years they've increasingly transcended them. This is an upside of living in an ideological age—or a downside, depending on how you see things. And those who bemoan the current polarization need to ask themselves whether polarization isn't the natural order of things. And, if it is—and I think it is—isn't this sort of polarization preferable to most of the other options?

8

Bipartisan Compromise Is Possible Despite the Political Divide

Kal Raustiala

Kal Raustiala is a professor of law at the University of California, Los Angeles.

Political polarization has increased in the U.S. Congress, but bipartisan compromises are still being reached on important issues. However, the nature of bipartisanship has changed. Formerly, most bipartisan compromises were reached between moderates of both parties; now, ideologues on both sides are finding unexpected common ground on moral issues, such as stopping prison rape and international sex trafficking, protecting the environment, and reducing oil consumption.

It is commonplace to claim that bipartisanship is dead—or at least dying. [On June 24, 2005], on *The New York Times* op-ed page, Norm Ornstein argued that political polarization is at a 50-year high in Congress. Ornstein showed that only 8 percent of the House can be considered centrist today, compared to 33 percent in 1955.

In light of Ornstein's findings, the first meeting of the National Prison Rape Elimination Commission, which took place in Washington [in June 2005], is puzzling—and noteworthy. Senators from both sides of the aisle spoke, and the commission heard testimony from activists, Justice Department officials, and rape survivors. The panel was created by the Prison Rape Elimination Act of 2003, which sailed through Congress ... with unanimous bipartisan support and was later signed by President Bush.

How, at a time when bipartisanship is said to be dead, did a bill addressing American prisons—a topic not lacking in ideological overtones—pass unanimously? The answer illustrates an important fact about bipartisanship in polarized times. The absence of centrists in Congress certainly fosters conflict rather than cooperation on many, probably most, issues. But there are also issues where the most liberal Democrats and the most conservative Republicans can find common ground. To be sure, that politics makes strange bedfellows is not news. What *is* news is that the rising power of the religious right is leading to some unexpected victories for progressive causes. Deep political polarization makes traditional centrist bipartisanship treacherous. But, paradoxically, it can also produce unexpected cooperation between the core of the right and the core of the left. In other words, bipartisanship isn't dead; it has simply abandoned the political center for issues where it was once nowhere to be seen.

Bipartisan Cooperation

The Prison Rape Elimination Act (PREA) is a good example of this phenomenon. Sexual assault, sometimes by guards but more often by other prisoners, is a fact of life behind bars. Research shows that nearly 1 in 10 male inmates has been raped, gay men disproportionately. The problem of prisoner rape is not new, but the issue had no traction for decades. Starting about five years ago, however, prisoner rape began to get attention.

In 2001, Human Rights Watch released a report on rape behind bars that was prominently featured on the front page of *The New York Times*. At the same time, the survivor-founded group Stop Prisoner Rape initiated a campaign that forced 7UP to pull a television commercial making light of the issue. Many conservative groups signed on to the campaign, including the evangelical Prison Fellowship Ministries, led by Watergate-era figure Chuck Colson. The media attention to both events dovetailed with ongoing work on the issue at the conservative Hudson Institute and coverage in publications such as *Christianity Today*.

Deep political polarization makes traditional centrist bipartisanship treacherous. But, paradoxically, it can also produce unexpected cooperation between the core of the right and the core of the left.

Conservative religious groups, many of which minister in prisons, witnessed the problem firsthand. More traditional conservatives recognized a law-and-order problem they could attack. And the fact that much of the sex in question was male-on-male surely added to the right's indignation. For the left, prison conditions have long been a concern—and a losing cause. But once Christian conservatives joined forces with groups like Amnesty International, the topic went from a political loser to a political winner. On conservative talk radio, advocates still faced hostile questions. But on Capitol Hill, few wanted to come out against a campaign that had garnered support from both the NAACP [a liberal civil rights group] and Focus on the Family [a conservative organization] [Left-wing senator] Ted Kennedy and [right-wing senator] Rick Santorum suddenly were on the same team.

The Bipartisan Trend

The PREA is an important story, one in which an appalling problem is finally addressed by Congress. But it is also part of a trend. In recent months, for example, the unusual convergence of the religious right and environmentalists has received increasing attention. "Creation care" is the new phrase *du jour* for environmentally minded Christians who think there is a scriptural duty to protect the Earth and all its inhabitants. Christian conservatives have also aligned with the left to campaign against the international sex trafficking trade. Conservatives are increasingly in line with liberals on the need to aggressively challenge and prevent religious and racial persecution in places like Darfur [Sudan]. And perhaps most significantly, national security hawks and climate change advocates are suddenly on the same page with regard to fossil fuel consumption—since, in addition to creating greenhouse gases, American consumption of oil also enriches Saudi Arabia, birthplace of fifteen of the 9/11 hijackers.

It's easy to argue there is nothing new in these coalitions. Prohibition is frequently said to have had two chief political supporters: Baptists who hated demon drink and bootleggers who smuggled it to everyone else. Whether or not that particular story is apocryphal, alliances of convenience—that is, "Baptist-bootlegger" coalitions—are hardly unusual in American politics. But the prison sexual assault issue pushes beyond these traditional kinds of arrangements. Rather than linking advocates of conscience (Baptists) to those seeking private gain (bootleggers), it connects advocates of conscience from opposite ends of the political spectrum. And in doing so, it reaches much further across the aisle than bipartisan efforts generally have.

When Christian conservatives . . . can partner with Amnesty International to push through a bill, bipartisanship is not so much dead as transformed.

This unusual brand of bipartisanship stems as much from the creation of gerrymandered electoral districts as it does from the rising power of the religious right. Congress lacks a center because the public, divided into ever-more homogenous and safe districts, no longer elects centrists.

The implications of this shift for congressional politics are significant. Our constitutional structure has a status quo bias that forces compromise if new initiatives are to move forward. Bipartisanship used to be more or less synonymous with the political center, where those compromises were forged. But the alliances that have formed around prison rape, the environment, and Darfur suggest that today it is less the center than the poles that are most likely to be areas of common cause. When Christian conservatives such as Chuck Colson can partner with Amnesty International to push through a bill, bipartisanship is not so much dead as transformed. In a sense, this is unsurprising: The center, as Ornstein tells us, has withered away. Bipartisanship has nowhere to go but out. This may make strange-bedfellow arrangements hard. But it can also make *very*-strange-bedfellow arrangements surprisingly easy.

9

America Has Always Had Divisive Politics

William Schambra

William Schambra is the director of the Bradley Center for Philanthropy and Civic Renewal at the Hudson Institute.

The level of divisiveness and nastiness in American politics is no higher now than it has been throughout American history, and it is no more of a problem now than it was in the past. The American democratic system was designed to deal with these inevitable divisions among voters, and historically it has done so quite well. American citizens should remember this and resist political reforms that would supposedly cut down on divisiveness by letting scholars and other elites, rather than average voters, control policy discussions.

"Let's step on them!" exhorts the early 1950s Republican election poster hanging in my basement. It features the party's pachyderm with his foot planted squarely on two squirming figures, one a mustachioed Stalin look-alike labeled "Communism," the other a spectacled, briefcase-toting bureaucrat labeled "New Dealism" [Democratic president Franklin Delano Roosevelt's political philosophy].

Whenever I hear the complaint that today's politics has reached unprecedented levels of nastiness, I recall that poster from what was supposed to be a "golden age" of politics, brimming with civil discourse, bipartisanship, and national unity. In fact, politics for our parents' "greatest generation" was just as boisterous, nasty, and over the top as it is today—indeed, as it always has been, for Americans.

Nasty Politics of the Past

Why? Because our democracy is grounded in realistic expectations about how politics would be conducted, once the rule of the "enlightened" few gave way to the sovereignty of the everyday person. The Founders believed, as James Madison noted in Federalist No. 10, that "So strong is this propensity of mankind to fall into mutual animosities, that where no substantial occasion presents itself, the most frivolous and fanciful distinctions have been sufficient to kindle their unfriendly passions and excite their most violent conflicts."

The idea is that democracy would liberate individual self-interest and narrow political ambition to an unprecedented degree, thereby skewing our politics toward a fairly low common denominator. But the Founders believed that our dispersed, decentralized political institutions could harness and counterbalance this crude political energy, moderating it and directing it toward some semblance of the common good.

Politics for [the] 'greatest generation' was just as boisterous, nasty, and over the top as it is today—indeed, as it always has been, for Americans.

Our nation's politics has seldom failed to live down to these humble expectations. As David and Johnny Johnson note in *A Funny Thing Happened on the Way to the White House*, our presidential contests have always been marked by scurrilous charges, innuendo, and outright lies.

Andrew Jackson was described by his opponents as a drunkard, bigamist, adulterer, gambler, and murderer. Abraham Lincoln likewise was viewed as an "awful woeful ass," a "dictator," a "coarse vulgar joker," and a "grotesque baboon." To Republicans in 1884, Grover Cleveland was a "lecherous beast," an "obese nincompoop," and a "drunken sot." But through all the calumnies and distortions, we have selected decent, if not always excellent, presidents, whose virtues were maximized and vices minimized by mutually vigilant, separated powers of government.

The History of Political Reform

Almost as enduringly American as nasty politics, though, is complaint about the nastiness of our politics, and efforts to reform it. The desire to tame partisanship characterized the civil service reform movement after the Civil War, as well as the "Mugwump" rebellion against corruption during the [Ulysses S.] Grant administration.

But concern about the baseness of American political discourse grew to a fever pitch at the turn of the 20th century. That era's "Progressive Movement" aimed to shift political power out of the hands of corrupt local political machines, into the hands of newly emerging national professional elites—university and think-tank scholars, philanthropists, enlightened federal administrators, and journalistic intellectuals. Their training and status, they argued, enabled them to take a detached, objective, superior view of the public good. A new "enlightened few" had emerged with a claim to rule, albeit in the best interests of the unwashed masses.

The Dangers of Reform Efforts

Over the past century, this spirit prompted innumerable reforms in the way we select presidential candidates, always in the name of fine-tuning popular rule, always with the effect of further enhancing the influence of the worthy. Yet modern-day heirs of progressivism in universities, think tanks, and journalism continue to punctuate each new election cycle with complaints about a politics that is debased, trivial, and simplistic. They prefer a politics that soberly, rationally, calmly discusses the "real issues." Some "deliberative democrats" now even suggest that we set aside a nationwide "deliberation day" a week before the presidential election, when all Americans would gather in small groups at local community centers for enlightened discussion.

American politics has always been robust, edgy, overstated, and 'simplistic.'

Deliberative democrats tell us that "simplistic" partisan politics is no longer sufficient, because our problems—global warming, nuclear proliferation, the growing gap between rich and poor—have become complex, cosmic, and difficult to grasp. To a citizen more likely to be concerned about the quality of that school down the street, the abstract, distant, but apparently urgent problems identified by experts mysteriously, but inevitably, turn out to be comprehensible and solvable only by the experts themselves. They frame the range of reasonable options to be made available for public consideration, which are then to be discussed in the staid, dispassionate, professorial manner at which professionals excel. Ironically, for all their disdain for the Founders' politics of self-interest and ambition, today's progressives still practice it, only now concealed beneath the nonpartisan mantle of objective public-spiritedness.

Is incivility a new and growing threat to American politics? No. American politics has always been robust, edgy, overstated, and "simplistic." Today's much-bemoaned 30-second attack ads are surely no more irrational, emotionally provocative, or unfair than posters of elephants stomping on Communism and New Dealism, which are meant to be viewed as two peas in a pod, according to the postermaker.

Only in the eyes of certain elites is our politics today more than ordinarily nasty. And the solutions to that nastiness just happen to augment the influence of those very elites. Though they argue for a transcendence of the Founders' low expectations for American politics, even they live down to them. . . . American citizens should celebrate, enjoy, and throw themselves into the exasperating, wonderful spectacle of our presidential election.

And when they hear complaints about our debased politics, they should reflect on this lament: "The age of statesmen is gone. . . . God save the Republic . . . from the buffoon and gawk . . . we have for President."

That was the *New York World* in 1864, commenting on the renomination of Abraham Lincoln.

Organizations to Contact

American Enterprise Institute for Public Policy Research (AEI)
1150 Seventeenth St. NW
   Washington, DC 20036
(202) 862-5800 • fax: (202) 862-7177
Web site: www.aei.org

AEI is a conservative think tank that studies such issues as government regulation, religion, philosophy, and legal policy. AEI's publications include the bimonthly magazine *American Enterprise* and numerous books, including the Vital Statistics on Congress series.

Ashbrook Center for Public Affairs
Ashland University, 401 College Ave.
   Ashland, OH 44805
(877) 289-5411
Web site: www.ashbrook.org

The Ashbrook Center for Public Affairs at Ashland University is a research institute devoted to the scholarly defense of individual liberty, limited constitutional government, and civic morality. The center supports research in both domestic and foreign policy issues and holds a variety of conferences and seminars for students, high school teachers, and policy professionals. The center produces books, monographs, dialogues, and op-ed articles, and audio recordings of many of its conferences and other events are available on its Web site.

Brookings Institution
1775 Massachusetts Ave. NW
   Washington, DC 20036-2188
(202) 797-6000 • fax: (202) 797-6004
e-mail: brookinfo@brookings.edu

Web site: www.brookings.edu

Founded in 1927, the institution is a liberal research and education organization that publishes material on economics, government, and foreign policy. It strives to serve as a bridge between scholarship and public policy. Its publications include the quarterly *Brookings Review*, the Policy Briefs series of papers, and the book *Is There a Culture War? A Dialogue on Values and American Public Life.*

Cato Institute

1000 Massachusetts Ave. NW
   Washington, DC   20001-5403
(202) 842-0200 • fax: (202) 842-3490
e-mail: cato@cato.org
Web site: www.cato.org

The Cato Institute is a libertarian public policy research foundation dedicated to limiting the control of government and protecting individual liberties. It offers numerous publications on public policy issues, including the triennial *Cato Journal*, the bimonthly newsletter *Cato Policy Report*, and the quarterly magazine *Regulation.*

Center for Media and Public Affairs (CMPA)

2100 L St. NW, Suite 300
   Washington, DC   20037
(202) 223-2942 • fax: (202) 872-4014
e-mail: mail@cmpa.com
Web site: www.cmpa.com

The center scientifically analyzes how the media treat social and political issues as well as the media's impact on public opinion. CMPA's publications include the bimonthly newsletter *Media Monitor*, which reports on press behavior, and periodic reports on the press's coverage of campaigns and elections.

The Century Foundation

41 E. Seventieth St., New York, NY   10021

(212) 535-4441 • fax: (212) 535-7534
e-mail: info@tcf.org
Web site: www.tcf.org

This left-leaning research foundation, formerly known as the Twentieth Century Fund, sponsors analysis of many issues, including electoral reform and the intersection of the media and politics. It publishes numerous books and reports, including a weekly "Public Opinion Watch" that summarizes and analyzes recent public opinion polls.

Democratic National Committee (DNC)
430 S. Capitol St. SE
   Washington, DC 20003
(202) 863-8000
Web site: www.democrats.org

The DNC formulates and promotes the policies and positions of the Democratic Party. Its Web site includes information on party activities and campaigns.

Heritage Foundation
214 Massachusetts Ave. NE
   Washington, DC 20002-4999
(202) 546-4400 • fax: (202) 546-8328
e-mail: info@heritage.org
Web site: www.heritage.org

The foundation is a public policy research institute that advocates limited government, traditional moral values, and the free-market system. It sponsors research in numerous areas of politics and culture, including governmental reform and the role of religion in civil society. The Heritage Foundation publishes hundreds of monographs, books, and background papers.

Hoover Institution
Stanford University
   Stanford, CA 94305-6010

(650) 723-1754 • fax: (877) 466-8374

Web site: www-hoover.stanford.edu

The Hoover Institution on War, Revolution and Peace at Stanford University is a conservative public policy research center devoted to advanced study of politics, economics, and political economy—both domestic and foreign—as well as international affairs. The institution hosts world-renowned scholars and ongoing programs of policy-oriented research. Its many publications include *Weekly Essays, Hoover Digest, Education Next,* and *Policy Review.*

Manhattan Institute

52 Vanderbilt Ave., New York, NY 10017

(212) 599-7000 • fax: (212) 599-3494

Web site: www.manhattan-institute.org

The Manhattan Institute is a conservative think tank that supports and publicizes research on urban policy issues such as taxes, welfare, crime, the legal system, city life, race, education, and other topics. The institute publishes a wide variety of books, articles, opinion pieces, reports, and speeches, as well as the quarterly magazine *City Journal.*

The Pew Forum on Religion & Public Life

1615 L St. NW, Suite 700

   Washington, DC   20036-5610

(202) 419-4550 • fax: (202) 419-4559

e-mail: info@pewforum.org

Web site: pewforum.org

Founded in 2001, the Pew Forum seeks to promote a deeper understanding of issues at the intersection of religion and public affairs. It carries out research in several areas, including the influence of religion and religious groups on politics and public policy debates. Its reports and transcripts from its conferences and events are available on its Web site.

The Pew Research Center for the People & the Press
1150 Eighteenth St. NW, Suite 975
  Washington, DC 20036
(202) 293-3126 • fax: (202) 293-2569
e-mail: info@people-press.org
Web site: www.people-press.org

Formerly known as the Times Mirror Center for the People & the Press, the center is an independent opinion research group that studies attitudes toward the press, politics, and public policy issues. Results of its surveys are freely available on its Web site.

Politics Research Group
John F. Kennedy School of Government
  Cambridge, MA 02138
(617) 495-1402
Web site: www.ksg.harvard.edu/prg

The Politics Research Group at the John F. Kennedy School of Government, Harvard University, brings together Kennedy School faculty engaged in empirical and theoretical research related to politics. The group sponsors seminars on current research, disseminates faculty papers, and facilitates an ongoing faculty research workshop. Its Web site features a directory of working papers on a variety of political topics written by Kennedy School faculty.

Progressive Policy Institute
600 Pennsylvania Ave. SE, Suite 400
  Washington, DC 20003
(202) 547-0001 • fax: (202) 544-5014
Web site: www.ppionline.org

The institute, which is affiliated with the centrist Democratic Leadership Council, promotes a "Third Way" in politics—a new progressivism that falls between traditional liberal and conservative politics. The institute carries out research on a variety of public policy issues, including political reform. Its policy reports are available on the institute's Web site; opinion pieces by its scholars frequently appear in the Democratic Leadership Council's *Blueprint Magazine* and are also reprinted on the institute's Web site.

Public Agenda
6 E. Thirty-ninth St.
  New York, NY   10016
(212) 686-6610 • fax: (212) 889-3461
Web site: www.publicagenda.org

Public Agenda is a nonpartisan organization that conducts research into public opinion and policy issues. It advocates for better voter education, a more nuanced understanding of public opinion, and for dialogue and compromise on political issues. Its Web site features opinion columns, research articles, and a database of "Issue Guides" providing in-depth coverage of political and social issues.

Republican National Committee (RNC)
310 First St. SE
  Washington, DC   20003
(202) 863-8500 • fax: (202) 863-8820
e-mail: info@rnc.org
Web site: www.rnc.org

The RNC formulates and promotes the policies and positions of the Republican Party. Its Web site includes information on party activities and campaigns.

Bibliography

Books

Michael Barone and Richard E. Cohen — *The Almanac of American Politics, 2006*. Washington, DC: National Journal Group, 2005.

James W. Ceaser and Andrew E. Busch — *Red over Blue: The Elections and American Politics*. Lanham, MD: Rowman & Littlefield, 2005.

E.J. Dionne, Jean Bethke Elshtain, and Kayla M. Drogosz, eds. — *One Electorate Under God: A Dialogue on Religion and American Politics*. Washington, DC: Brookings Institution, 2004.

Morris P. Fiorina — *Culture War? The Myth of a Polarized America*. New York: Longman, 2005.

Thomas Frank — *What's the Matter with Kansas? How Conservatives Won the Heart of America*. New York: Metropolitan, 2004.

Stanley B. Greenberg — *The Two Americas: Our Current Political Deadlock and How to Break It*. New York: Thomas Dunne, 2004.

James Davidson Hunter and Alan Wolfe — *Is There a Culture War? A Dialogue on Values and American Public Life*. Washington, DC: Brookings Institution, 2006.

John B. Judis and Ruy Teixeira — *The Emerging Democratic Majority*. New York: Scribner, 2002.

Geoffrey Layman — *The Great Divide: Religious and Cultural Conflicts in American Party Politics.* New York: Columbia University Press, 2001.

John Micklethwait and Adrian Wooldridge — *The Right Nation: Conservative Power in America.* New York: Penguin, 2004.

Thomas E. Patterson — *The Vanishing Voter: Public Involvement in an Age of Uncertainty.* New York: Knopf, 2002.

Larry J. Sabato, ed. — *Divided States of America: The Slash and Burn Politics of the 2004 Presidential Election.* New York: Longman, 2005.

Mark Satin — *Radical Middle: The Politics We Need Now.* Boulder, CO: Westview, 2004.

John Sperling — *The Great Divide: Retro vs. Metro America.* Sausalito, CA: PoliPoint, 2004.

Jeffrey M. Stonecash, Mark D. Brewer, and Mack D. Mariani — *Diverging Parties: Social Change, Realignment, and Party Polarization.* Boulder, CO: Westview, 2003.

John Kenneth White — *Values Divide: American Politics and Culture in Transition.* New York: Seven Bridges, 2002.

Periodicals

Alan Abramowitz and Kyle Saunders — "Why Can't We All Just Get Along? The Reality of a Polarized America," *Forum,* vol. 3, no. 2, 2005.

Alan Berube and Mark Muro	"'Red-Blue America' Is Not Black and White," *Dallas Morning News*, May 14, 2004.
Molly Motley Blythe and Jeffrey Weiss	"Beyond Red and Blue," *Dallas Morning News*, August 17, 2005.
Louis Bolce and Gerald De Maio	"The Politics of Partisan Neutrality," *First Things: A Monthly Journal of Religion and Public Life*, May 2004.
Alan J. Borsuk and Nahal Toosi	"Focus on Values Drove Many Bush Voters, Polls Find," *Milwaukee Journal Sentinel*, November 3, 2004.
David Brooks	"Age of Political Segregation," *New York Times*, June 29, 2004.
Economist	"Politics as Warfare," November 8, 2003.
Thomas Byrne Edsall	"Blue Movie: The 'Morality Gap' Is Becoming the Key Variable in American Politics," *Atlantic Monthly*, January/February 2003.
William A. Galston	"A Victory for People Like Us: Moral Values and the U.S. Election," *America*, February 14, 2005.
Paul Glastris	"Perverse Polarity: The Mainstream Media Bemoans the Lack of Civility in Washington—But Won't Say Who's Responsible," *Washington Monthly*, June 2004.
James L. Guth et al.	"America Fifty/Fifty," *First Things: A Monthly Journal of Religion and Public Life*, October 2001.

James Harding   "Into the Heart of Suburbia," *Financial Times*, January 15, 2005.

Jerry Large   "Red and Blue Don't Define—Or Cleave—All America," *Seattle Times*, August 30, 2004.

Joseph Lelyveld   "The View from the Heartland," *New York Review of Books*, November 4, 2004.

John Leo   "Splitting Society, Not Hairs," *U.S. News & World Report*, December 15, 2003.

Alex Markels and Robert Zausner   "Angry in America," *U.S. News & World Report*, October 25, 2004.

Liz Marlantes   "Inside Red-and-Blue America," *Christian Science Monitor*, July 14, 2004.

Christopher Muste   "Hidden in Plain Sight: Polling Data Show Moral Values Aren't a New Factor," *Washington Post*, December 12, 2004.

James Nuechterlein   "What's Right with Kansas," *First Things: A Monthly Journal of Religion and Public Life*, March 2005.

Jonathan Rauch   "Bipolar Disorder: A Funny Thing Happened to Many of the Scholars Who Went Out into the Country to Investigate the Red-Blue Divide. They Couldn't Find It," *Atlantic Monthly*, January/February, 2005.

Jonathan Rauch   "In 2004, the Country Didn't Turn Right—But the GOP Did," *National Journal*, November 13, 2004.

Hanna Rosin   "Beyond Belief: The Real Religious Divide in the United States Isn't Between the Churched and the Unchurched. It's Between Different Kinds of Believers," *Atlantic Monthly*, January/February 2005.

Godfrey Sperling   "America Still Divided on Bush, but Less Bitter," *Christian Science Monitor*, March 8, 2005.

Stuart Taylor Jr.   "How the High Court and the Media Aggravate Polarization," *National Journal*, October 30, 2004.

John Tierney   "A Nation Divided? Who Says?" *New York Times*, June 13, 2004.

Jay Tolson   "How Deep the Divide?" *U.S. News & World Report*, October 25, 2004.

Matt Welch   "All Tomorrow's Partisans: The Culture War After the 2004 Election," *Reason*, January 1, 2005.

Alan Wolfe   "The Referendum of 2004," *Wilson Quarterly*, Autumn 2004.

Index